Week 2:

CD: The Power of Mindsets
CD: The Power of Thought and Visualization
CD: The Role of Positive Thinking
CD: The Law of Attraction vs. Your Thoughts

Week 3:

CD: The Power to Create Your Vision
CD: How to Think Like a Wealthy Person
CD: How Imagination Changes Us
CD: Preparing Yourself for Supernatural Dreams

Identity Network   P.O. Box 383213   Birmingham, AL 35238   205.362.7133

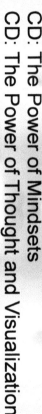

School of Thought, Visualization, and Imagination

Course Syllabus

Week 1:

DVD: Introduction
DVD: Create Your Day
CD: Manifesting Consciously What You Want
CD: What in Life Do You Really Desire or Want
CD: Keys to Mastering What You Want in Life
CD: Having the Life that You Desire
Booklet: The Power of Thought & Visualization

THE POWER OF THOUGHT AND VISUALIZATION

By Dr. Jeremy Lopez

THE POWER OF THOUGHT AND VISUALIZATION

By Dr. Jeremy Lopez

Copyright © 2013 by Jeremy Lopez

Published by Identity Network
P.O. Box 383213
Birmingham, AL 35238
www.identitynetwork.net
United States of America
The author can be contacted at
customerservice@identitynetwork.net

Book design by
Treasure Image & Publishing
TreasureImagePublishing.com
248.403.8046

CONTENTS:

As A Man Thinketh In His Heart

There is a lot of talk today concerning thoughts and visualization. In my personal life I can see where the power of thoughts has literally come into fruition, come into a place where it has materialized in my life. I know that thoughts truly become things. We see it from Christianity and see it carry over into every single religion on planet earth. We see it all throughout creation where people are beginning to recognize and take note in the power of thoughts and power of visualization.

The mind has the power of creativity, the mind can create things and thoughts become things.

Even within Christianity we see where the Bible says, *"As a man thinketh in his heart, so is he."* (Proverbs 23:7)

First of all, we have to realize that in this one phrase alone it is talking about the mind of man, not just Christians, but how every man *thinketh*. Therefore we are talking about a universal person, we are talking about creation; we are talking about a people, not a religion. This universal principle or law goes beyond religion and Christianity; it goes into the thoughts of every single person on planet earth.

"God hath dealt to every man the measure of faith." Romans 12:3

Jesus spoke about faith as a mustard seed in Matthew 17:20:

*"Verily I say unto you, **If ye have faith as a grain of mustard seed**, ye shall say unto this mountain, Remove hence to yonder*

place; and it shall remove; and nothing shall
be impossible unto you."

Every single person has been dealt the measure of seed-like faith. These passages of scripture show us that the thoughts of every human, no matter what he personally believes, holds power.

As a man, as a woman, as a Christian, a Buddhist, a Hindu, an Atheists, thinks in his heart, so is he. When you look throughout society at people, rich and poor, black and white, no matter who a person is, no matter what they do, no matter what their life style is, every person is governed by their thoughts. Many people do not understand the fullness of what I mean by our lives being governed by our thoughts. When we say things such as, *"thoughts become things,"* is this true or is this false?

According to the Christian faith, we see it as being true.

7

"As a man thinketh in his heart, so is he."
Proverbs 23:7

"A good man out of the good treasure of his
heart bringeth forth that which is good…
for of the abundance of the heart his mouth
speaketh." Luke 6:45

I am established in my life according to what I think because what is on the inside of me is what is going to be projected on the outside. What is inside of me is going to come out of my mouth, therefore what I eat spiritually is going to be what I begin to display and project.

Casting Down Vain Imaginations

"Casting down imaginations, and every high thing that exalteth itself against the knowledge of God, and bringing into captivity every thought to the obedience of Christ;"
2 Corinthians 10:5

The Bible says that we should cast down every vain imagination. We need to take captive every thought that is contrary to the Christ conscious mind, the mind of Christ, the mind in which we are to behold, the mind in which we are to possess, and the mind of which we are called to take a hold.

The mind of Christ speaks of a higher way of living. This is a place of salvation, and an entrance to the door of the heavens where we are called to live and move and breathe.

*"He is not far from each one of us; for in
Him we live and move and have our
being…" Acts 17:27-28*

It speaks of a place where it focuses upon
things that are good and pure and holy and of
awesome report.

*"Finally, brethren, whatsoever things are
true, whatsoever things are honest,
whatsoever things are just, whatsoever
things are pure, whatsoever things are
lovely, whatsoever things are of good report;
if there be any virtue, and if there be any
praise, think on these things."*
Philippians 4:8

In this mindset you are positive and at a
place in your life where there is a continual
win-win situation.

*"And the Lord will make you the head and
not the tail; you shall be above only, and not*

be beneath..." *Deuteronomy 28:13*

"For whatever is born of God overcomes the world. And this is the victory that has overcome the world: our faith. Who is he who overcomes the world, but he who believes that Jesus is the Son of God?"
1 John 5:4-5

So the mind of Christ speaks of overcoming. It speaks of victory. It speaks of being the head and being on top of the game.

When the Word of God talks about casting down every vain imagination, or taking every thought captive, what does that mean exactly? It means to take charge over any thought that is contrary to the perfected life, anything that is contrary to the abundance of life, and anything that is contrary to things that are of good report.

Your focus should be on thoughts that are pure, things that make you rejoice, make you cheer, and things that put a smile on your face.

Anything that enters your mind that is contrary to the mind of Christ, to His thinking, emotions, or a Christ-like lifestyle, have to be consciously cast down and gotten rid of. Get rid of it because it is considered an enemy of positivity, happiness, prosperity, joy, and living an abundance of life.

Jesus said in John 10:10,

"I am come that they might have <u>life</u>, and that they might have it more abundantly."

That more-abundant life is the greek word *zōē*. *Zōē* is the eternal, everlasting life of God, or *"the God kind of life."*

When you have *zōē*, you cooperate with God, and become co-creator of your own life. People do not seem to realize that they are the creators of what they become due to how they believe and think.

Do I have control of my own personal life because of what God in heaven has displayed and given to me? Absolutely! Do I control, ultimately, my destiny? Absolutely! Do you have control if you grab a gun and shoot someone? Do you have the control or power, or does God? Do you not have the control and power to put a smile upon your face?

> *"And if it seem evil unto you to serve the Lord,* **choose you this day whom ye will serve***, whether the gods which your fathers served that were on the other side of the river, or the gods of the Amorites in whose land ye dwell. But as for me and my house, we will serve the Lord." Joshua 24:15*
> *"I call heaven and earth to record this day against you that I have set before you life and death, blessing and cursing.* **Therefore choose life, that both thou and thy seed may live;***" Deuteronomy 30:19*

Everything in life is based on choices we

make, and we as sons and creators have the power to paint a picture of our own life, to create and paint what we want our lives to be.

You can choose positively or negatively, but the choice is ultimately yours. God can override things if He chooses.

He is the God of positive thinking and the God of life and joy. He wants us to be like Him. He speaks things into existence by *calling those things that are not as though they were*. (Romans 4:17).

God is delighted in us when we think as creators of our lives and say, "I choose to have money," "I choose to be healthy," or "I choose to eat the right foods." A lot of times we don't look at our own lives when we have certain things that come upon our body.

Can you control your obesity? Absolutely! Can you control what you eat? Absolutely! Can you control when you sleep? Of course!

You have the power to control these situations in your life because the heavens and the universe of which God is the creator has given to us (in Him), the power to choose life or choose death, the two opposite extremes that everyone will face.

I want to break it down into scriptures to help you understand how powerful visualization is, how powerful thoughts are in our lives and how they govern and rule our lives.

What I think about today will ultimately turn into the actions and decisions that will bring me to my future. If I continuously ponder and think about pornography, if I continuously lust over someone, is it not true that I will begin to attract people of the same kindred spirit, the same way of thinking?

Is it not true if I ponder and think upon something negative that I will begin to attract negative people? Absolutely! If I deal drugs and I'm constantly thinking, pondering, meditating, focusing, living, and acting upon my thoughts of taking and selling drugs, what will happen?

The universe will begin to bring those same types of people, under Gods command, that I will be able to do the drugs with and sell the drugs to. Drug dealers hang out with drug dealers. That's why people with lust issues will begin to hang around with other people that have lust issues.

Creation (The Universe) Is Groaning For The Manifestation Of The Sons Of God.

Look at society. It is evident that the wealthy neighborhoods are separate from the impoverished. When is the last time you saw a multimillion dollar mansion beside a trailer park. When is the last time you saw an apartment complex beside a castle? When is the last time you saw multimillionaires living right next door to someone who brings in maybe $20,000 a year and lives in a trailer or an apartment? You won't see this situation because even in the natural there is a breaking down and separation of people who hang out with like-minded individuals.

Thoughts create and produce your life,

and how and with whom you surround yourself.

> *"For the earnest expectation of the creature waiteth for the manifestation of the sons of God. For the creature was made subject to vanity, not willingly, but by reason of Him who hath subjected the same in hope, because the creature itself also shall be delivered from the bondage of corruption into the glorious liberty of the children of God. For we know that the whole creation groaneth and travaileth in pain together until now." Romans 8:19-22*

This passage speaks about how creation moans and groans and travails, waiting for the manifestation, which means the replacement or the repositioning of the sons of God. Creation moans and groans so that we can see that creation actually has thoughts. Creation actually has a mind.

God never says that He waits for the

manifestation of the sons of God. It never said that the Holy Spirit waits upon us. No, it says creation. You are talking about a substance that God created and has empowered it with a mind to think produce emotions.

This shows me that creation has a thought process. Creation has a mind, will, and set of emotions. Creation has thoughts of moaning, groaning, rejoicing and happiness. The moans and groans of Creation are a result of it waiting for the root positioning, shifting, and replacement of the sons of God to be where they need to be.

Therefore, it is saying that people need to be in their God-appointed place at the right time. Creation is powered by our thoughts. It is empowered by its desire for God's people to take their place as the head and not the tail, to begin to manifest in having a *Zōē* kind of life, living the God kind of life, and wanting the best out of life. Creation has thoughts and emotions. When creation is down and depressed, moaning and groaning, it is due to seeing a people that is not rising to be the very best in life, not being successful, and not taking on the heavenly mindset.

The Christ-conscious mind understands all that one is called and created to become and complete for God.

Therefore, creation has emotions and a mind to think. Creation longs for the sons to begin to come forth, manifest, and be their very best. Another word for creation is cosmos, or universe, which means one body or one mind. When you hear people say that the universe is moving on their behalf, there is nothing wrong with this thinking. Creation has a mind and emotions that is under God's control.

If people have the power to choose life or death then the universe must move and respond upon the thoughts of the people of

God, and upon the thoughts of humanity. We are talking about Christians, about man, about universal beings, about humans. Therefore as I think, as humanity thinks, the universe responds to the thoughts of every single person on planet earth.

Thinking Specific Positive Things And Projecting It Into God's Universe

The ultimate place God wants us to be is where we have a Christ-like mind. Knowing we are the head and not the tail, and moving out of positive thinking, in the Zōē kind of life, and moving into the destiny of what we are called to do. I am led by the Spirit, and when the Holy Spirit begins to lead me it means that in my life as a creator I create my destiny by the thoughts in which I think.

Again, I am called to think about things that are true, honorable, right, pure, lovely, and of a good report. (Philippians 4:8). Therefore, if I don't think with my mind on heavenly thoughts then I begin to get the opposite, whether I am thinking positive or negative.

Psychologists have estimated that, on average, we have as many as 60,000 thoughts per day. Can I control 60,000 thoughts a day? Absolutely not! But can I begin to walk in a place of awareness where I focus on thoughts that are true, honorable, right, pure, lovely, and of a good report? Yes!

Think about being full of grace and mercy. Giving my heart away, giving my money away, and giving my life away in service of someone else. I want to constantly have thoughts about empowering other people no matter if I work in ministry or not. Whether I write books, whether I am an executive or a janitor, I should learn to control my thinking and live in a place of awareness where I can say, "I want to be able to think positive and to project that to the universe." To say, "I can change lives." First you have to ask.

"Ask, and it shall be given you; seek, and ye shall find; knock, and it shall be opened unto you." Matthew 7:7

How do I ask? I first must think the thought. If I think of something that I need from God, then I ask. Seeking God is the corresponding action behind my faith leading me to knock. This brings you to the place of Omega giving you the boldness to say, "This is what I've been thinking about and pondering on. I want to be an author. I want to be able to have a ministry that touches people's lives. I want to be able to walk in grace." Those are great desires, but you need to be very specific with God. For example, "I want to be a bestselling author. I want to change *this* person's life. I want to change *these* people and *this* specific city. I'm called to the black culture, or the white culture, I'm called to these people."

Maybe you want to own your own

business. God will ask details, "What business do you want to own?" It may be you owning a Chik-fil-A, or a corporation. I want to knock on the door of being a publisher. I want to knock on the door of the thoughts I am thinking of being a bestselling author. I want to knock upon the door of opening my own restaurant. I want be an accountant and this is how I want to do it. I want to direct my skills and knowledge towards churches. I want to empower them, and provide them with better avenues to save more money. You have to learn to be specific in what you ask. You also have to be specific in your thought process. You need to cast down every vain imagination.

Imagination is visualization. Therefore anything that is contrary to being ahead in life and being a creator has to be cast down because it is not worthy enough for you to think upon. You have to cast those negative thoughts down and say, "You are not worthy enough to be in my brain. I cast you down because the mind of Christ says something totally different."

Let's think about the story of Moses in Numbers 21:8.

"And the LORD said unto Moses, Make thee a fiery serpent, and set it upon a pole: and it shall come to pass, that every one that is bitten, when he looketh upon it, shall live."

This story shows how powerful visualization is. The people had been bitten by snakes and God said to take the same creature that bit them, put it on a pole and use it to reverse the curse. God wanted to take that same visual picture that once brought fear to them and turn it around for His glory and their good. What does it mean to behold? It means to see, to visualize, to imagine, or to create. So as I address thoughts that once were negative and fearful for me, look upon that circumstance that once hurt me, and now shift it in my mind and look upon it and empower it in the positive.

Now this is a key factor that you need to realize. I have the power as a creator to shift my thinking and visualization from fear to positive. God's instruction essentially says, *"The same thing that once hurt you will now heal you."* So as the people viewed the snake upon the pole it brought healing to them and no longer brought fear. The people came into agreement and said, "I shift by beholding something now that was once harmful for me.

I shift my mind of thinking and now view it as positive. Now I allow it to bring healing to me." That is how powerful you are. That what you behold you become and what you visualize will begin to manifest in your life. Thoughts become things. If I think about the snake on the pole, it is going to bring me healing and begin to manifest in my life. Why? Because God willed healing and restoration to take over my mind and body, and because God used creation, the universe, to bring these to me. It is ultimately up to me to behold it, visualize it, and to allow healing and restoration to take over my mind and my body.

Choose Today To Visualize The Positive; To Visualize God As The Good God

You empower whatever in life you are beholding. Whatever you behold in life you have the power to shift from being either positive or negative. The power of the Creator allows this. The Creator is Elohim, which means creator or creators since it is plural. This does not mean that there are multiple gods. It means it is a plurality of the big G and the small g's, which we are. Psalms even records that we are small gods to God.

"I have said, 'Ye are gods, and all of you are children of the Most High.'" Psalm 82:6

Therefore, this does not mean anything new age. That is what it means according to scripture, that God is God and we are the small creators, or small gods.

> *"His divine power hath given unto us all things that pertain unto life and godliness, through the knowledge of Him that hath called us to glory and virtue."* 2 Peter 1:3
> *"For the Lord God is a sun and shield; the Lord will give grace and glory; no good thing will He withhold from them that walk uprightly."* Psalm 84:11

God says, **"I've given you all things that pertain to life and godliness. No good thing will I withhold from those who walk uprightly."** I am empowered with all good things because I have the fullness of God living inside of my mind.

Therefore I have to be careful what I think, what I behold, what I see, and what I ponder upon. As discussed, whatever I behold I empower. A lot of people back in the old Pentecostal days, through much ignorance and lack of knowledge, did not go to movies because they viewed them as being evil. You have to realize that knowledge is power, and as you become empowered to understand this line of thinking, you begin to see all things as being good as opposed to seeing them as evil.

We know there are things and movies out there that are bad for you, but when Jesus is Lord of your life and not just Savior, you begin to see Him in everything instead of always seeing the bad.

If your mind is trained by focusing on demons, evilness, devil and hell, you will see the negativity in everything.

"Unto the pure, all things are pure; but unto those who are defiled and unbelieving, nothing is pure, but even their mind and conscience is defiled." Titus 1:15

As a person begins to train his mind to see Christ as Lord over his life, versus a way of escape, then he will begin to see life in a whole different light. What happens is you will begin to see things as being pure, and will begin to find the Christ in everything.

Laughter Is A Good Thing

"A merry heart doeth good like a medicine,
but a broken spirit drieth the bones."
Proverbs 17:22

When I watch something comical, such as something funny on television, I begin to laugh. Therefore I begin to apply the medication of laughter and a merry heart to my life, bringing wholeness and healing to my life. Why? Because *laughter works like a medicine.*

"And Abraham was an hundred years old,
when his son Isaac was born to him. And
Sarah said, 'God has made me to laugh, so
that all that hear will laugh with me.'"
Genesis 21:5-6

Abraham was 100 and Sarah was 90 when

their son was born. God's promise made them to laugh, which actually healed their physical bodies so they could bear a son at their old age! They even named their son Isaac, which means "Laughter." As I begin to walk in the mind of Christ, I begin to walk in purity. All that I behold I can be viewed as evil, bad, and horrible or I can behold the positive things, and the promises of God, and find principles and ideas in something that I can begin to think about, ponder on, and let change my life for the good.

Choose To Visualize The Positive; Visualize God As A Good God

You have a place in your life where you have the power to choose to utilize your creative power. Because you have creational powers as an Elohim to say, "I choose this day to find the good in my situation. I choose this day to see the positive in people." It is the same with prophesying and with preaching.

When you have a bad outlook on your own life and you see God as judgmental, mean, horrible, vengeful, then you begin to project that image upon yourself. How you view God is how you view yourself.

If you view God as a loving, awesome, powerful Creator who loves His people, and sees the good in them, and desires them to have a good life then you will begin to take that as healing upon yourself and see yourself as having those same characteristics.

Consequently, when you begin to see yourself this way, you will begin to prophesy and project this thinking to other people.

You will have a visualization of a God who loves you. You will begin to behold the true, awesome, living God, and will begin to receive and accept it for yourself.

You will find yourself thinking, pondering, meditating, and having visualizations of God being a good God. And then when you prophesy to others you will prophesy that same precious faith, that same love, that same tangible grace and mercy, and compassion towards other people.

A person might prophesy doom and gloom and see the bad in people. They may see when someone is in adultery.

They may view this in the lowest part of their spirit, only focus on the bad part about that person and begin to prophesy those negative thoughts. They begin to knife folks and cut them up. It is because they have that same imagery of God doing that in their own life. I try to teach people to begin to find out who God is first.

When you define God and find out who He really is and who He is towards you and towards His creation then you will begin to be that to other people. If not, then stay out of the pulpit and do not preach and prophesy.

"Every good gift and every perfect gift is from above, and cometh down from the Father of lights, with whom is no variableness, neither shadow of turning."
James 1:17

You must have a good visualization of

who the Father is. He is the Father of lights. Lights mean illumination.

"But the path of the righteous is like the light of dawn, which shines brighter and brighter until full day." Proverbs 4:18

Therefore, as you realize that the path of the righteous gets brighter and brighter and becomes illuminated more and more, you will discover how good, awesome, and amazing God is.

"No good thing will He withhold from them that walk uprightly." Psalm 84:11

This scripture helps us understand that God is a good God who displays good things towards His people. You begin to see Him in this light and illumination, in other words as love. When you understand God's character you begin to display and show it towards other people.

Therefore you will be liked and will draw people that are good, nice, loving, generous, and kind to yourself because you are putting off that air. You are putting off the same energy as God.

Energy, Light, And The Projecting Of Energy By One's Associations

Once again here is another word that confuses people: energy. Can a word be religious? Can a word be new age? No! Can a word be Buddhist? Can a word be Christian? Absolutely not! A word is just that, a word. Whoever takes hold of that word has the power to empower that word. How they see it, how they portray it, how they behold it, how the visualize it, and how they think about it is what it becomes.

What is energy? What does it mean? Science will tell you that everything in creation is nothing but a vibrating energy. You are energy.

Then spoke Jesus again unto them, saying,
"I am the Light of the world. He that
followeth Me shall not walk in darkness, but
shall have the light of life." John 8:12
"You are the light of the world. A city that
is set on a hill cannot be hidden. Nor do
they light a lamp and put it under a basket,
but on a lampstand, and it gives light to all
who are in the house. Let your light so shine
before men, that they may see your good
works and glorify your Father in heaven."
Matthew 5:14-16

Jesus is the Light of the world, and He also said that we are the light of the world. We are a light set upon a hill that cannot be hidden. Therefore, what is energy?

Energy is pure light. Science even backs this up and you can always back up the Bible with science if you look deep enough. I am nothing but pure energy. So, was God right in saying I was light in the spirit? Absolutely! Because I am pure light and so are you. Do not let people freak you out or scare you when they use the word energy. We even project heat off of our bodies.

Suppose that you are in a room with five or six people that are in a really bad mood and you have to work with them all day. They are constantly being negative, and are talking about how much they hate their job, how much they hate life, and how their family lives are horrible.

If I sat here and talked to you an hour about how horrible life is, and how life never deals me a good hand and I am never joyful because everything goes wrong, and you were surrounded by that kind of negative talk you would become just like that. You are going to find all of the negative and all of the bad in everything you encounter. Why? Because I am giving off a bad vibe. I am giving off bad energy.

All that means, once again is that err of

projecting and beholding what they have beheld in their own thought process. I was projecting negativity and it came upon you. That is why you have to keep your mind pure before the Lord and focused on good things.

Produce For Yourself A Win-Win Situation

There are so many scriptures that will empower you. For example, the story in Genesis 29 of Laban and Jacob.

Jacob worked for Laban for seven years in order of having the privilege to marry his daughter, Rachel. Laban tricked him into marrying his other daughter, Leah. So Jacob had to work another seven years to get the sister that he wanted.

Laban, being Jacob's father-in-law, acting as if he was full of remorse for the trick he played on Jacob, told Jacob that he was going to reward him for his fourteen years of hard work. He told Jacob that all the cattle that was spotted he would give to him.

There was not a whole lot that were spotted. So Laban knew for him it was a win-win situation.

Beholding What Lies In Front Of You

Right now in your own life, the circumstances around you may show you that life is not good for you. You are not doing well, you are never going to be on top, and you are not making a lot of money at your job, because you only have "a couple spotted calves." You look at your circumstances and think negatively that it looks like a lose-lose situation. You are going downhill. Laban looked at the situation and said it was a win-win situation.

Begin to be empowered with the knowledge that the law of attraction in the universe works, because God set it into motion just like the law of gravity. The law of gravity has nothing to do with religion. The law of gravity is not Christian, it does not speak in tongues, it is not Catholic, is not Buddhist, and is not Muslim.

The law of attraction and law of gravity are universal laws that God has placed into the universe that respond to the people of God. The law of gravity responds to humanity across the board whether they are religious or not, Christian or atheist, no matter who you are. Christian, Buddhist, Muslim, or atheist, when a person jumps off of a building the law of gravity does not care who you are, what you do, or if you are a good person or a bad person. You will hit the ground! It is a universal law that works for humanity.

It's the same with the law of attraction, with a minor difference. The law of attraction does not care who you are, what you do, or what you think and believe. It focuses and functions according to what God has placed inside of it to go into motion. Therefore, the law of attraction works. There are millions of people that do not understand their thought process and their visualization. They suffer from a lack of knowledge. They do not understand and realize their lack, and they come to a place where negative things happen to them because they are constantly meditating and pondering on it. They do not know to turn their thinking around for something good. They do not realize that they can turn their stinking thinking around into something positive.

Since the law of attraction works regardless then I might as well let it work for my good and for God's glory. I want to be the head and not the tail, so I have to start focusing on this marvelous business I am going to have, this wonderful ministry, and give it details of what I want. Creation moans and groans waiting for the manifestation. The universe is waiting on you to give it some ammo. It is waiting on you to speak to it, give it instruction, and is waiting for direction of what area or part of life you want it to go towards. With every thought you, creation is going to say, "Your wish is my command. I will go and do that for you. You want to be broke since you are saying you are broke, so I'll help you get there." The universe does not care if you think positive or negative. It simply goes off of the thoughts in your mind. Therefore it is so important to understand this principle that Jacob understood the power of thoughts and the power of the law of attraction.

"And it came to pass, when the stronger cattle did conceive, that Jacob laid the bark before the eyes of the cattle in the feeding troughs, that they might conceive among the bark." Genesis 30:41

Whenever the stronger females were in heat, which means they were ready to conceive, Jacob would place the bark in the troughs where the water was to drink so that they would mate near the branches. When they would come into heat they would see the bark that was in their trough as they drank from it. The whole time they were drinking they were subconsciously seeing the bark floating in the water. When you put things into water, like the bark, it looks like spots. So what they beheld, they produced. Jacob understood principle of 'thoughts become things.' A person having no clue of what is going on would never think about this or imagine this.

But a person who knows the law of attraction, who understands the principles that whatever you behold even creation itself understands. I get a mental picture of you having brown hair, no hair, or blonde hair; you are short, tall, or skinny. I now have a visual picture of you that sticks in my mind. Therefore if you are 400 lbs. and I do not see you for three or four years, then to behold you again I am shocked to see you have lost 200 lbs. I am shocked because you have changed the visual in my brain. The image that has been ingrained in me because I have meditated on what you looked like has changed and does not remain the same.

That is why we are shocked as humans because our minds are so powerful. Like a camera, our minds take pictures of things. When those things begin to change, our minds are shocked because our mental picture is being challenged. Jacob knew the concept that if he placed the bark in the water that when the cattle would conceive that the universe would create a shift in their bodies and begin to cause every cell to line up and produce or create spots on their young.

Then, when they came forth in the earth, they would have spots. That is how Jacob won, because he used visualization to win this situation. So for him it was a win-win situation. When you begin to realize the concept of what you think and what you behold you will begin to manifest. It is time for you to realize, as you get this concept, your life will be a win-win situation. Does it mean your life will be perfect? No. Does it mean you will not go through hard times and troubles? No. It means you will begin to get a mental picture of whatever the end result will be.

"Declaring the end from the beginning, and from ancient times the things that are not yet done, saying, My counsel shall stand, and I will do all my pleasure." Isaiah 46:10

God knows the ending from the beginning. So God wants you to get an end picture of what your destiny is going to look like. You have to decide what you want.

*"**Choose you this day whom ye will serve…**" Joshua 24:15*
*"**Choose life, that both thou and thy seed may live;**" Deuteronomy 30:19*

I choose a life of victory. I choose to serve a life that God has given to me, which is a life more abundant. I choose to serve a destiny where I come out on top. I come out the head and not the tail, a winner, a champion. I come out attracting people to the books I will write one day because it will shift their life, because my goal is to become a bestselling author.

My visual picture is to become a bestselling author that will change society and humanity, not just Christians. To live a better life, to be prosperous, healthy, whole, and to experience the God kind of joy that God has for them. I get that projection or imagery and see the end result of that.

So what happens in my life?

Since I have an image of an end result of what I am after, I begin to ponder on that and never let it leave my mind. I continue to let it magnify in my mind and let God expand the borders of my imagination. Then it is God's job to cause the creation of the universe to shift and say, "This is the desire of his heart.

This is what he desires and what I want for him."

Anything in life that comes from a place of grace, mercy, giving, victory that will empower and better humanity, God is for that. You have to realize that whatever avenue or goal that is for you as an individual you have to choose that. And as it lines up with what He has for you and you get a mental picture of His vision, never let that thought go. Thoughts produce things and thoughts become things and it will happen for you one day. You will begin to produce the spotted cattle, but you have to put the imagery and thought out there and continue to hold the thought.

I continue to hold the thought of the bark in the water of the trough of my life, because what I behold I will become. You begin to get that in your mind. Look at the story of Abraham and Lot, where God had promised Abraham a new land to go to. Abraham had taken his nephew Lot with him and they traveled together.

But on the road God spoke to Abraham and told him to separate himself from Lot. If you look in the Hebrew, you see that the name Lot means *"veil or covering."* Therefore Abraham could not behold the land that God had for him until he removed the negative image, or the veil or covering, that was keeping him from seeing the land. To see what God had for him, Abraham had to remove the veil.

There are a lot of "Lots" and veils and coverings in our lives obscuring the view of God's promise. I like to call those negative thoughts or negative "how's" because people say, "How am I going to do this? How can this be achieved? How can this be accomplished?"

Remember in Luke 1:26-38 when the angel announced to Mary that she was chosen to bear the Son of God; Mary asked, *"How can this thing be? How can I get pregnant knowing that I have never been with a man? How can I bare forth a child when in the natural laws it is not humanly possible?"* The angel reassured her with the promise of God, which gave her peace and faith to say YES to God and to her destiny.

You have to get rid of the *how's* because the *how's* will curse you. You should never ask, "How can this thing be? How can this happen?"

Because the cursed *how's* will destroy your thoughts, your destiny, and your vision because they limit you to natural reasoning. They will destroy the visual images in your mind because the images are placed there and as you behold them they will produce that thing that you want. If they are not vain images or imaginations that you cast down and they are not negative to your destiny then you behold them and meditate on them and you begin to see them produce.

You have to get rid of the cursed *how's* and say, "It is not about the *how's*, it is about the thought process and focusing on the prize." Then you make your way towards the prize and God will align your entire life to where you will be able to meet the right person at the right time at the right place. No matter what it takes, He will get you to the place you need to be. He sees the end result of what you are projecting, thinking and desiring. You have to push your desire as much as you can.

You have got to have passion for that desire. Push your passion into the end result of your life. Whatever the end result is you have to think of yourself as happy. When you look at your own life no one can make you unhappy unless you empower them to make you miserable. You have the right to be happy and the right to be sad, and you have the power in you to choose.

Against all the odds, against all the situations you are facing in your life you can choose to be happy. Does it make sense, even if you are going through something in your life or it seems like nothing around you is winning, to feed into that and empower it more by thinking negative or being miserable? Or does it make more sense to recognize the situation or circumstance and choose not to give in to it and to empower it. Because bottom line is you can live in a place of misery.

Let's say you are in a place of misery that goes on for a three-year span. You could receive it, allow it, and accept it and run with it by visualizing it and accepting the thoughts of that situation of your life. You can allow it to impregnate you with more misery and depression because you see and recognize and come into agreement with your bad situation. Or you can say, "This is obviously how it is right now in my life, but I am going to change the way I am thinking. I am going to begin to focus upon things that are good, awesome, pure, and begin to smile." Then you will see the situation of the three-year span start to change.

Why? Because you begin to change the situation in your mind and focus on the good things and the joy. All of a sudden the universe, through the law of attraction, begins to shift and change your thinking process. It begins to cater to the new way of thinking. No matter what you are thinking, positive or negative, good or bad, it does that for you. Creation says, "I'm not moaning and groaning anymore," because it recognizes that you are beginning to manifest, replace, and reposition yourself as a son of God, to think like a son of God, and to be a son of God.

All of a sudden Creation gives in to the positive and instead of moaning and groaning it begins to lighten up and be joyful. It recognizes that you are beginning to act like God. You are beginning to awaken as a good creator and to create a positive destiny. When you do that you will find that everything will begin to shift and that situation or circumstance will shift from something negative to something positive.

Before you know it, your life will be on top and you will not even realize how you got there. God will say, "Because you chose to think like me. Therefore I began to move on your behalf." The mind is so creative and so powerful. It is very important that you begin to take an inner look into your life and your thinking and make the change in your life today.

Choose to decide what you want in your life today, what you want in your life tomorrow, what you want in your life next year, and even ten years from now. Do not say to yourself, "I do not know where I will be. I do not know what I will be doing. I do not know if I will have the money."

You need to get rid of all the cursed *how's* and begin to realize no matter what you are doing in your life it is going to be good, it is going to be great, and it is going to be joyful. You are changing your thinking and focusing on the end result. However long it takes you to get there you need to rejoice in the journey of life. Through the journey you are going to learn, gain knowledge, begin to advance, meet people, network, and travel.

Yes, you will hit hard times but you need to keep thinking positive and keep being on top. Realize you are changing your life around because sometimes you will go through hard times and God will say, "Are you reacting or responding?" You need to respond by constantly shifting your mind to think because you realize that thoughts become things.

The more you shift your thinking to say, "It does not matter. I am going to keep on going because one day I am going to be a bestselling author. I am going to own my own business. One day I am going to be a great missionary. One day I am going to be an awesome motivational speaker. One day I am going to be a producer in Hollywood. One day I am going to be the best actress." You focus and you do not deviate from your thoughts and what you want in your life.

And God, through His divine ultimate love and His divine will for your life, will begin to shift to make sure you get to the Omega of your life. He will shift you to make sure that everything that you go through will be a learning process to empower you on the way of your journey. So when you do meet your destination it will begin to manifest for you and you will look upon the journey of your life and say it was worth it. Everything you went through made you a better person to reach your destiny.

On the way of your journey God will begin to connect the dots. The universe will connect the dots for you to meet just the right people. Sometimes you will meet people along the journey that are not the nicest people. You will still embrace it because somewhere in your life you thought that into existence. Somehow you are learning through the will and sovereignty or God how you are going to face those kinds of people. Somehow in your life God will say, "I need you to face this because you can't get to your destiny until you go through this thing." And as you begin to go through this situation, you will shift your mind to focus on the destiny and not what is going on now."

In 1 Kings 13 we find a story of a prophet that had received strict orders while delivering God's message, *'You shall not eat bread, nor drink water, nor return by the same way you came.'*

However, along the road he deviated from his journey because he came across a lying prophet that said, "*Come back to my house and eat with me.*" And he got in trouble, and lost his life because he did not do what he was told to do.

You have to find your destiny, find the end results, and do not let anyone cause you to deviate from that. When people try to cause you to deviate from the path of your destiny, bless them and love them and go on. You have to learn to keep your eye on the prize and keep your eyes focused on the destiny that has been set before you.

God desires for you to have the *Zōē* kind of life. Remember the principle, thoughts become things. Your life is a product of what you have been thinking about all the days of your life. Whatever you thought about two years ago is probably manifesting right now in your life. All the mean things you have said about other people could be why you are now facing a situation where people are being mean back to you. The same love you displayed to someone else years ago could be the same love God is about to bring to you in your life because you need it.

The same thoughts you thought ten years ago that say, "One day I want to really learn. I want to get deep revelatory things of the Bible." That might be why you are receiving this message at this very moment because you feel in your spirit God saying, "This is what you need to hear right now to get you to the next level of your life." God will orchestrate your life, even like a movie in Hollywood. Movies are created sometimes with the big finale or the ending at the beginning. When you watch a movie you watch it in the time frame that it is set up to be. You watch the beginning, the middle, and the end and you see it in that sequence.

But sometimes directors will make it choppy. They will create the ending first and they will lead back to the beginning, or the beginning may be halfway through, or all the way to the end. Your life is like that. You begin to focus first on the end result, the grand finale of where you are going to be in your life. Then let God orchestrate through creation everything in your life; the patterns, the cycles, the timeline, and the sequence of how it should be set up for you to get the end result of your life.

Bio of Dr. Jeremy Lopez:

Dr. Jeremy Lopez is Founder and President of **Identity Network International, Sounds for Now, Awakening to Your Now** and **Now is Your Moment.** Identity Network is a prophetic resource website that reaches well over 153,000 people around the globe and distributes books and teaching CD's. Jeremy has taught and prophesied to thousands of people from all walks of life such as local church congregations, producers, investors, business owners, attorneys, city leaders, musicians, and various ministries around the world concerning areas such as finding missing children, financial breakthroughs, parenthood, and life changing decisions.

Dr. Jeremy Lopez is an international teacher and motivational speaker. Dr. Jeremy speaks on new dimensions of revelatory knowledge in scripture, universal laws, mysteries, patterns, and cycles. He has a love for all people and desires to enrich their lives with love, grace and the mercy of God and to empower them to be successful.

Dr. Jeremy believes it is time to awake the Christ Conscious mind and live out the victorious life that was meant for us. His desire is to live a life filled with purpose, potential, and destiny. He ministers with a revelational prophetic teaching gift that brings a freshness of the word of the Lord to people everywhere.

This is accomplished through conferences, prophetic meetings, and seminars. He serves on many governing boards, speaks to business leaders across the nation, and also holds a Doctorate of Divinity. He has had the privilege of ministering prophetically to Governor Bob Riley of Alabama. He has also ministered to thousands overseas including millionaires around the world. He has traveled to many nations including Jamaica, Prague, Paris, Indonesia, Haiti, Hong Kong, Taiwan, UK, Mexico, Singapore, Bahamas, Costa Rica, Puerto Rico, etc. He has hosted and been a guest on several radio and TV programs from Indonesia to New York.

He is the author of nationally published books, 'The Laws of Financial Progression,' 'The Power of the Eternal Now' (Destiny Image) and his newest book, 'Releasing the Power of the Prophetic' (Chosen Books). He has also recorded over 45 teaching CD's.

Jeremy's ministry has been recognized by many national leaders and other prophetic leaders around the nation.

For more information on Dr. Jeremy Lopez, please visit DrJeremyLopez.com.

Dr. Jeremy Lopez has many books, ebooks, audio downloads, and teaching CDs for you to enjoy and to grow.

OTHER PRODUCT BY DR JEREMY LOPEZ:

Books:

The Power of the Eternal Now (book) by Jeremy Lopez

The Laws of Financial Progression (book) by Dr. Jeremy Lopez

Releasing the Power of the Prophetic: A Practical Guide to Developing a Listening Ear and Discerning Spirit (book) by Jeremy Lopez

Made in the USA
Charleston, SC
16 January 2015